5 TIPS *for*
SPIRITUAL SURRENDER

WORKBOOK

By

Judith Anne Winters

AWINEE
Publishing Company

All rights reserved Published by AWINEE Publishing Company, Los Angeles
ISBN: 978-1-7322463-1-7
Judith Anne Winters

Table of Contents

Dedication

This book is dedicated, first to Spirit, the muse of my life. I am grateful for my clients who inspired me to listen and learn from their transformations. I am grateful to my family and friends who supported me with encouragement and love during the scared incubation period and finally the birth of this idea.

Introduction

Welcome to YOUR Workbook. This workbook may cause you to feel uncomfortable but you have landed in the Spiritual Surrender Series for a good reason. Sometimes we want to feel a new experience which takes us out of our comfort zone. New experiences are a dynamic process of moving forward.

Follow these steps to use the workbook . I recommend that you form a partnership or group to read the book and follow the workbook exercises.

Divide your time together into weekly discussions; set a time to gather; or just do it yourself! Most of all have fun!

Chapter 1

Awakening to My Authentic Self

The discovery of who you are requires looking inside and feeling with the heart which is the most sensitive and important aspect of the self.

How do you manage the Ego and the Higher Self? There is no requirement to manage them.

I learned, through my years of searching for balance and harmony in my life, that they are the same. Let me explain.

I learned that my ego keeps me safe from harm. It is an alarm system within my physical body that alerts me when there Is danger in my environment. It also alerts me when I feel discomfort.

As a small child I learned to feel the danger or comfort within my body. It all began in my stomach or gut as it is so called. As I grew older, this altering system became cumbersome. I did not enjoy the feelings of discomfort.

Hence, I strove to keep my mind and body in a state of harmony. The magic is to find a balance and allow both to do their function. Without balance, there is conflict.

❖ Stand before a mirror and look at yourself. What do you see?

_____

_____

❖ Describe what you see in one to two words.

_____

_____

❖ Use this word to identify yourself, by saying I AM.

_____

_____

❖ If the word was **WISDOM** , repeat to yourself, **I AM Wisdom** If you did not identify a word, then return to the mirror and look at yourself until a feeling provides you with a word.

> *"Today I am a reflection of God's Love."*

❖ Become aware of this feeling and word throughout your day.

Practice Exercise

Before falling asleep, place your hand over your heart region and repeat several times, **I AM LOVING MYSELF.** Do not think about the words. Just repeat them. You will fall into a deep sleep. When awakened in the morning, repeat: "Today I am grateful for my LIFE".

Describe your feelings below.

_____

_____

_____

_____

_____

_____

_____

_____

_____

_____

_____

_____

_____

_____

_____

_____

_____

_____

_____

_____

_____

_____

_____

> *"Today I AM grateful to feel the Beauty that surrounds me."*

Chapter 2

I AM

What holds your attention? You are energy. You are the creator of your reality. Focus on beauty, and you see and feel beauty. Focus on chaos, you see and feel chaos.

Practice Exercise

Become aware of your surroundings. What do you see?

_____

_____

_____

_____

_____

_____

_____

_____

_____

_____

_____

_____

_____

_____

_____

_____

_____

_____

_____

_____

_____

_____

_____

_____

_____

_____

Identify one object or person of Beauty and declare your Gratitude by saying: **I AM Grateful for** :

_____

_____

_____

_____

_____

_____

_____

_____

_____

_____

_____

_____

_____

_____

_____

_____

_____

_____

_____

_____

_____

_____

_____

Repeat the steps until you feel the gratitude.

> *"Today I Listen and Obey"*

Chapter 3

Stillness and Listening

(How to become still and listen). You are constantly in a state of move-ment, except during times of sleep and death.

It takes courage to become still.

However, the courage to be still is already within you. Your body knows how to do this, but the mind needs to be trained.

Practice Exercise

Meditation Sit in a chair or on a floor pillow in a quiet place where no one can disturb you. With hands on your knees, palms turned upward, and eyes closed, begin to breath in on "1" and out on "2".Relax the body. Eyes closed, gently turn your eye focus upward and feel a shift of Vision inwardly. Concentrate on breathing. If your mind wanders, bring it back to your breath.

Focus : Hold your attention on breathing; then listen for the still small voice of Spirit. You will hear the voice. Allow it to speak to you. (Start agin if your mind wanders.)

Write about this experience below.

What did you feel? What did you hear? What was your message? It may come to you as a word, voice, color. (Spirit speaks to me in a variety of ways.)

_____

_____

_____

_____

_____

_____

_____

_____

_____

_____

_____

_____

_____

_____

_____

"Trust Intuition IT does not lie."

Chapter 4

Trusting the Message

Did you ever have a feeling in the pit of your gut that something was happening? Intuition is calling. It is the messenger. Trust that your body signals according to your belief. Yes, belief is everything.

Practice Exercise

Take off your shoes and walk barefoot on MotherEarth. Allow your feet to feel an energetic sensation flowing from your toes to head.

Write about this experience below:

Where does it land in the body?

What is the message?

Describe your feelings

_____

_____

_____

_____

_____

_____

_____

_____

_____

_____

_____

_____

_____

_____

_____

_____

_____

_____

_____

_____

_____

_____

_____

_____

_____

_____

_____

_____

_____

_____

_____

_____

_____

_____

_____

_____

_____

_____

_____

_____

_____

_____

_____

_____

_____

_____

_____

_____

_____

_____

_____

_____

_____

_____

_____

_____

> *"I AM Loving Myself, God, and all life forms."*

Chapter 5

I AM Loving

Love is a verb in action. Loving is energy flowing between you and another, person, place, or thing.

Practice Exercise

Gather a sheet of paper, pen, pencil or crayons and draw a heart shape on the paper.

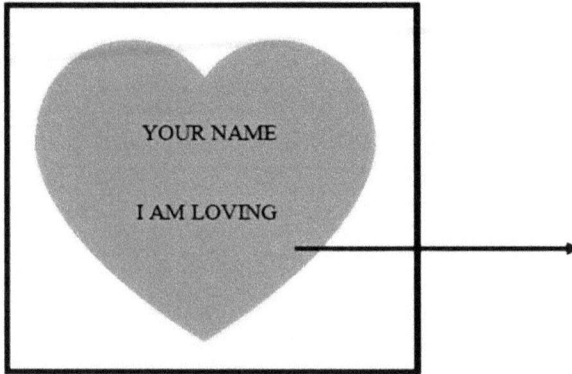

Write your name in the center of the heart image. Below your name write in bold letters **I AM LOVING** then draw lines from this phrase to the names you write on the outside of the heart. Don't forget to Begin with YOU and GOD/SPIRIT. When you feel complete, stop and review your master piece.

How did you feel about giving love?

Are you Grateful?

Tearful?

Joyful?

Uplifted?

Describe below your feelings about loving others.

_____

_____

_____

_____

_____

_____

_____

_____

_____

_____

_____

_____

_____

_____

_____

_____

_____

_____

_____

_____

_____

_____

_____

_____

Repeat the above steps but this time you write within the heart image "I RECEIVE LOVING FROM".

Then list the names of people, places, events that give you love as the arrow/energy flows back to you.

I RECEIVE LOVING
FROM

Write below your feelings about receiving Loving.

_____

_____

_____

_____

_____

_____

_____

_____

_____

_____

_____

_____

_____

_____

_____

_____

_____

_____

_____

_____

_____

_____

_____

_____

_____

_____

_____

At the end of your day, read your thoughts and feelings about Loving. Read them aloud to yourself; if you like stand or sit before a mirror and look deeply at your reflection.

Repeat **"I AM LOVING ME NOW . I AM LOVING GOD NOW. " "I AM GIVING AND RECEIVING LOVE."**

By repeating the phrase you are a vibrational energy of unconditional love. It is done to you according to your belief. FEEL, ACCEPT AND KNOW your truth. You are powerful as the Living Presence of the Divine.

Congratulations! You did it! You have stepped into your greatness as a Spiritual Being of Light and Love. If you did not complete the practice exercises, there is no judgment. Take your time and go back to areas that you may have skipped or did not complete. NOW is your sacred space and time. The practice examples are here for use when you are ready. There is no 'completion'; only expansion of your consciousness as a new self- image. You will know when expansion begins. It will be a feeling you have never experienced before. For each step you take on this path of enlightenment, enjoy the ride. You are here; you are now; and you are home.

About the Author

Rev. Dr. Judith Anne Winters is an ordained minister, Doctorate of Divinity, and Agape Licensed Spiritual Counselor. She is a master seminar leader, master alchemist, and master of transmutation. She is founder and Spiritual Director of Spirit of the Earth Ministry. Rev. Judith shares her gifts with the world as a Spiritual Intuitive and Transformational Life Coach.

Ode to the Creator

Light breaks the dawn
A gentle swirl of air envelops the space
Silence is the stillness of the moment
Whispers gently brush the treetops
As raindrops gently fall slowly to the ground
Rainbow colors permeate the sky
Awe and wonder dance like twins
When darkness births a new beginning.
It is Good; Very Good.

Redhawk, 1985